Still Life with BOTTLE

WHISKY ACCORDING TO
RALPH STEADMAN

Ɛ̓

EBURY PRESS
LONDON

Acknowledgements

There are Art Directors and then there are Directors of Art, and then again Art, Directors of. They are all useless and I loathe their meddling in my attempts to fill a vacuum as self-indulgently as is humanly possible. They leech on to the essence of your idea and then claim it as their own. That is what they get paid for. They also get paid for putting as much distance between an author and his creation as is possible, without resorting to physical violence, in order to preserve the sanctity of office life inside a publishing house. They are known to a few of us exclusive authors as book bouncers. However, once in every generation one comes along who is not only a brick but who excels in every aspect of . . . but I digress. My thanks to IAN CRAIG, Art Director of my whole life, who once again has bound me to the mast, blocked my ears against the wail of tempting sirens and steered me clear away from the rocks of my own blind folly.

Editors are in the main loathesome jelly, slimy moss on rocks, accumulated fluff from beneath a restless spirit's mattress, and on occasions the scrapings from a great man's dandruff. But, once in every last decade of a millenium, one wanders in out of the desert and rewrites the Bible or something and expects to get paid for it as well. Operating from a bedsit above a launderette in Lyme Regis and trading under the unlikely handle of GORDON KERR, Private Investigator, I had hired him to keep an eye on my wife but caught him looking through my papers and trying to cook his head in the microwave. I could tell he had literary aspirations when he asked me if I kept a thick red pencil about me. So I let him loose on my bulky manuscript, the undistilled ramblings of all my investigations into moofling vapours euphaungulating through the mists of time. With commendable ferocity he went through it like a combine harvester in overdrive. However, copies of the full unexpurgated text of my deepest imaginings can be obtained from the above premises in Lyme Regis, or would have been if the fool hadn't trashed the whole lot in the wastebasket of my Scottish Macintosh Performa 400 in a fit of Jacobite pique. Being Scottish himself, he sided with the Macintosh machinery, taking exception to the flippant attitude he believes I have adopted towards a subject that obviously means far more to him than keeping an eye on my wife.

DENISE BATES, or Dennis as she is affectionately known, is in fact a code name for Operation 160, the systematic restriction imposed on all would-be authors who tend to go on a bit and who would waste vast amounts of publishers' money which otherwise can be put to better use whipping up needy book reps into a selling frenzy at conferences in posh hotels. Operation 160, or Editorial Director to give her the second code name she uses, takes the oil out of turmoil and skilfully uses it to lubricate the wheels of creativity. She holds the reins and drives the wayward energy through a narrow gap, miraculously steering it towards a hopeless deadline, urging it ever onward, until the creation, now wheezing like a damp bagpipe, is taken by the scruff of the neck, stamped on, and printed in time for publication.

ANNA, my wife, who as always saves the hours like rare butterflies and lets them fly inside our lives. She gently guides the silly away into the sunlight of their own making, and helps the time-wasters to light up the shadow of their squander. Deeply involved with her own creations, she nevertheless has time to listen as I groan my thoughts out loud through a bullhorn. She helps to give them form more than she could know. Forever patient . . . how *does* she do it?

Special thanks to JOHN HUGHES at Matthew Gloag, MATTHEW GLOAG himself, JIM MCEWAN at Morrison Bowmore, WILLY MCNEILL at Glen Garioch, and the many kind distillers, blenders, coopers, malters and smugglers who must have wondered what the devil I was up to.

Hardback edition first published 1994

This paperback edition published 1996

1 3 5 7 9 10 8 6 4 2

First published in the United Kingdom in 1994 by Ebury Press, Random House, 20 Vauxhall Bridge Road, London SW1V 2SA

Random House Australia (Pty) Limited
20 Alfred Street, Milsons Point, Sydney,
New South Wales 2061, Australia

Random House New Zealand Limited
18 Poland Road, Glenfield,
Auckland 10, New Zealand

Random House South Africa (Pty) Limited
PO Box 337, Bergvlei, South Africa

Random House UK Limited Reg. No. 954009

A CIP catalogue record for this book is available from the British Library.

Hardback ISBN 0 09 178409 3
Paperback ISBN 0 09 1820243

Design: Ian Craig

Typeset by Textype Typesetters, Cambridge
Colour separations by Magnacraft, London
Printed and bound in Italy by New Interlitho Italia S.p.a., Milan

Contents

INTRODUCTION 5
The Making of Whisky 8

*WILD WILLY GLENGARGLE was shot in
the bag and deflated between the
Cumlorden retreat and the Gay Gordons. It
was a terrible loss of wind throughout
Scotland. It took three visits to Macklo
Cuskie's wee burn bothy to revive the
deflated parts . . . (an obscure old snippet of
an account of obscure origin).*

Ian Fyfe has worked at Glen Garioch distillery since 1956 and treated me to a private performance of some of his old bothy songs in the reception area referred to as The Bothy. He was accompanied only by Glen Garioch's 10, 15 and 21 year-old malts. He never forgets a single word and starts up the moment you are seated with a glass in your hand, as though he has just been wound up and switched on . . .

BOTHY SONG by IAN FYFE

Noo doon in a wee toon in Buchan
Ah practised fur mony's a year
Every man they said socht
For ye now tae yer horse
He's lookin' a wee bittie queer

Noo I noticed his stirk
In the new tatty park
Wi his tail up and lugs hangin doon
Noo he said
Tell the foreman tae get on his bike
An get the best vet in the toon

Ae nicht wi ma gig an ma shetty
I wid dauner an hame afore dark
An ah hid a wee dram maybe een
Maybe twa
An ah saw a man coming through the tatty park

Cried a fine night
An he never took heed
But ah fun oot in the day
A'd been wasting ma wind
On a scarecrow stuck up in a drill.

IAN FYFE SINGING BOTHY BALLADS ON THE UNACCOMPANIED 10, 15, and 21 YEAR OLD!

Introduction

A tale of desperate longing, thirst, deceit, ingenuity, violence, plagiarism, common theft, betrayal, over-indulgence, duty, death and destruction. A litany of bad behaviour, secrecy, monopolies, mists of despair, outrage, penury, butchery, lechery, savagery and bagpipe karaoke. A history of sorts – an illicit romance . . .

A whisky trail can take you on a hard and dangerous journey. Aye, it can be a slippery slope, an uphill climb and a Pandora's Box of quaint behaviour and weird moments. Going into training for such a daunting task is more a trial by abstinence than of reckless indulgence. Single malt whisky is a drink to be respected, treasured, savoured, and even kept for half a lifetime, if necessary, to avoid it being trashed on an oblivious palate. It is neither a drink to quench a thirst, nor merely a drink to look at for very long, when the sun is going down. It fulfills all of these requirements and more. It gathers momentum with every passing year. It fires dreams in the depths of despair and it gathers stories inside itself, as rich and dark as an ancient peat bog.

'tis a dark bottle so that it does not look ugly when half empty.'

Only a Celt could have said something so pessimistic and yet so saturated in soulful longing for something not yet finished but sadly, now, only half the friend it was. The apparent simplicity of the statement masks a deep, entrenched and tormented philosophy that life must be hard no matter how good it appears to be, and if it is really good, then there is surely pain around the corner. And he is right of course.

But it is whisky I am writing about here, so I have no business getting bogged down in the dribbling self-pity of a Scotsman in his

cups. The problem is – and I can vouch for this, after much sojourning in the MacHighlands, the MacLowlands, the McGlens, the Burns and the Lochries – you cannot separate the one from the other, and maybe that is the miracle of it all.

This book will probably float about everywhere like the very vapours that moofle off the bubbling wort in every pot still from here to Ballindalloch and back to Tennessee, but never mind, so long as it gives you, along the way, a taste for the 'Cratur' itself. The spirit, and the rich diversity of its nature, is the thing.

I could never pretend to have seen it all, much less even taste it all, but what modest amount I have seen *and* some of the things I have not seen, I will share with you, like the

rude imaginings of Scottish gossip. Even though they did not invent distillation, the Scots invented the poetry that makes whisky what it is.

Yet it was not always so. To separate the deadly union of self-righteous Calvinism from a god-fearing, guilt-ridden and compulsive alcoholic claim to their very own drink, I must first go down the road of my own choosing in search of any clue to the whereabouts of the first process.

In this world, nothing unique is anybody's in particular, it seems to me, and anybody who says otherwise is a usurper and a charlatan, which includes just about everybody who made a fast buck out of a good idea. It seems to depend on who was in the right place, with the right conditions, at the right time and managed to catch their piece of luck in full flood, as it were, and then flew by the seat of his or her pants until the opposition lost interest, fell by the wayside or was even exterminated. And don't dismiss that as the way of all things either. It is merely a Darwinian theory, but it can work in business, too.

The Grain of Truth

A gnarled industry, deeply bitten and scarred in rich folklore. Feastie Tales, dark as peat, rich and warm as copper stills. Steaming wort and fermenting wash, wafting through the ether like fairy-tale demons. Aye! The stuff of a smuggler's secrecy, distilled from native cunning and filtered through time. The wild, warm inner fire of natural strength. The story of whisky is a saga of human nature versus bureaucratic control. The wisdom of old country ways, trial and error, ingenuity, spirit safes, padlocks, wild extremes and perfect balance.

A whisky blender of years' standing develops a nose saturated to bursting and yet a sixth sense evolves and pierces the plethora of aromas like a steel spike nailing every nuance to its mast. It is probably the nearest a human being will ever get to emulating the homing instinct of a salmon, swimming up-river to breed.

What I imagined of whisky distilling, distilleries, regions and traditions and the reality of what I saw, were pretty close.

It is true that while a very skilled and scientific approach is observed in the making of whisky, there is still something very homely and rule-of-thumb about the whole process, which charmed my own artistic skill to the core. These are native ways I am talking about and what goes on beneath the kilt is no more mysterious than what goes on inside a copper still. This is alchemy of a high degree and it is no accident that these weird tubular objects of desire take on the characteristics of strange beasts and creatures from the time when hobgoblins and wizards cast spells and curses abroad like black confetti and ruled the dark areas of people's thoughts with the restricting fear of the unknown. Beneath this veil the heart of whisky was born, and it is no accident that it was so.

The early whisky distillers needed the very cover of darkness to mask their activities from the hooded eyes of excise men and their willing flunkies, the gaugers. These registered zombies roamed the Highlands and the Lowlands, like lost souls in Purgatory, searching for the liquid gold that was needed to line the coffers of the English throne, waging wars in foreign lands. Colonialism was a fever as deep-seated as the desire of the Gaelic soul to keep out the cold; and these forces matched each other face to face for supremacy.

The English won, of course, not because they were right, but because brute force and the English gentleman's god-given right to everything he claps his eyes on subdued the Scottish right to self-determination which, amongst other things, ushered in the Whisky Excise Act of 1823.

Although the Scots Parliament imposed considerable duty on whisky in 1644, it was in 1707, after the Union of the Parliaments, that the English Revenue Officers were allowed to cross the border. They attempted to control the rampant whisky distilling that was as much a part of Scottish tradition as hating the English. And so the trouble began.

It became a code of honour to make illicit whisky and it was a badge of honour and a blow struck against the English throne to drink it. It was also a nonsense to distillers and smugglers, all good men and true, that they should actually pay the sworn enemy for the privilege of making their own national drink, and a process that was as natural to them as it is now for the English to make jam and green tomato pickle. The travesty stuck in the throat of fervent patriots who realised that the duty paid, at hopelessly divergent rates, went to finance English land-rape worldwide – the Scotsmen rightly rebelled.

Even after a Royal Commission brought in the 1823 Act to stamp out the wild and rebellious practice of rampant distillation, true Scotsmen continued to insist on a smuggler's dram. It appears to make honourable, just and perfect sense. The Englishman's arrogant imposition was an abberation, and still is. The claim to this duty is probably illegal even today, but that's another story, and a claim I can only make here, since I think it would be foolish and futile to pursue it in the courts. Mind you, if there is a law student out there with enough balls to make it the subject of a thesis, who would I be to argue with him or her?

On the island of Islay, with 4,000 inhabitants on a piece of land 25 miles long by 20 miles wide, the 7 distilleries provide the British Government with 150 million pounds of duty annually. The people of Islay could, if they felt inclined, pull up the ladder and be self-sufficient, setting up their own principality, as prosperous and independent as Monaco, and screw the British Government. But instead the money is pissed away on foreign diplomatic mismanagement and every other government slush fund, by a Westminster long gone on rhyme or reason.

The first significant distiller to go legal was George Smith, grandson of a Bonnie Prince Charlie supporter, John Gow, who had changed his name to plain ole John Smith, to protect his family from the filthy wrath of the English after the Battle of Culloden. John became a farmer and whisky distiller but never went legal. His grandson, George, reckoned that legitimate distilling was the industry's future. He was encouraged in this thinking by his landlord, the penniless but land-rich Duke of Gordon, who stood to make good money from the sale of the grain grown on his land, which Smith transformed into poetry and liquid assets. Consequently, George Smith was a turncoat in his fellow distillers' eyes. He became a controversial figure and was obliged to keep two pistols at the ready, day and night, for fear of reprisals. His company still flourishes under the name of The Glenlivet, in the Grampian Highlands of Speyside.

The Cairn at Aberfeldy by the TAY – Freedom of Booze Black Death – 4/9 93

The Making of Whisky

But how is whisky made, this magical potion, this rare yet prolific nectar? Well, it is full of secrets we can never understand, but I *can* tell you how to make it. And why not? Who are these suits who thrash about spoiling it for others . . .

Basically, it is the simplest of culinary principles, couched in the old-fashioned ways of keeping the pot going on the hob and adding rich complexities of fresh new ingredients to an older brew. At least, that is how I perceived the origins of the process. It was probably an accident and maybe even goes back before the first known recorded reference to 'bolls of malt

enzyme diastase is produced in the barley during germination, which converts it to starch and sugar solubles. This is called 'Green Malt'. *YOU can simply spread yours on newspaper and turn it with your fingers, every hour on the hour, over a lazy weekend.*

Germination is halted by drying the converted barley in a malt kiln, a kind of pagoda-shaped tower, with a peat fire down below, allowing the smoke to rise up through the drying-floor which is covered with the barley, and then out into the open air through the pagoda-shaped chimneys. This process gives the raw material its peaty flavour. *YOU can achieve this on the average garden barbeque, using garden refuse, old leaves, peat moss etc. to*

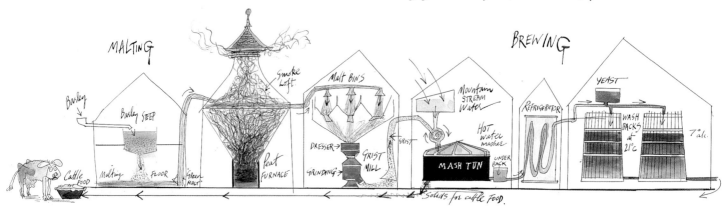

to Friar John Cor wherewith to make aquavitae', in the Scottish Exchequer Rolls of 1494. Probably old porridge, accidentally distilled on a reboil in a sock, oozed through an outlet pipe, under an ice-cold Highland stream, into an old leather sporran. A lost wandering Celtic Christian missionary may have spent his last words triggering the ingenuity of some restless, thirsty Scot with magical gibberish, of weird practices he had witnessed on board a junk on the South China Seas and Och aye Bingo! – the recipe was born.

The ingredients are *that* simple. Barley and pure, soft, Highland water bubbling over granite through peat, and yeast.

The barley goes through a malting process. It is steeped in water for two or three days, drained off, spread across a large stone or concrete malting floor and allowed to germinate. The germination is often controlled by determined Scottish insomniacs, ploughing it continually over a period of 8 to 12 days. The

smoke your grain dry, spread out on sheets of metal colander gauze.

The malt, now dried, is ground into grist, through a maroon-painted grist mill, still made by an engineering company called Porteus, who have made the same mill for over one hundred years. The resulting grist is mixed with hot water in a large circular tub called a mash tun. The soluble, powdery starch dissolves into a brownish, sugary, half-boiled liquid called wort, which is then drawn off, leaving behind husky solids. These husky solids, draff as they are now called, are used for cattle food. *YOU can use your kitchen blender on a slow speed, and use the discarded solids as compost nutrients.*

The wort is piped into a huge washback – another tub, which can hold anything from 9,000 to 45,000 litres, and is made of wood or, more frequently now, of stainless steel. This is fermented over a period of about 48 hours, with the addition of yeast at a temperature of around 21 degrees – 'the age a woman is at her most awkward,' as a Scottish misogynist said. The liquid, unattractively called wash, is now at about 7 degrees alcohol strength. The rest is still water and impurities. *YOU can use a plastic dustbin and maintain the temperature near a radiator in the hall, whilst the yeast goes to work and ferments the wash.*

Distillation takes place by boiling the wash in a copper still, shaped like an alchemist's retort. Alcohol boils at a lower temperature than water, and thus evaporates before the water does. The alcohol level of the distilled liquid rises to about 23 degrees in the vapour, which condenses into a liquid state, through a cooling plant of coiled pipes in cold water

ered whisky and it is still colourless. The rest, called feints, the tail of the distillation, is recycled and re-distilled, together with subsequent batches of wash and low wines, in skilfully balanced ways. It is this process which brought to mind the old country habit of the perpetual hot-pot over the open fire. What went before enriches what comes after and nothing is wasted, which to a Scotsman is second nature. Perhaps that is the real secret of the Scots' ability to produce the best malt whisky in the world – thrift.

Only when it has lain in oak sherry-casks, in a damp, cool cellar for at least three years, would a Scots' distiller presume to call it whisky. By then it will have lost any sharp-

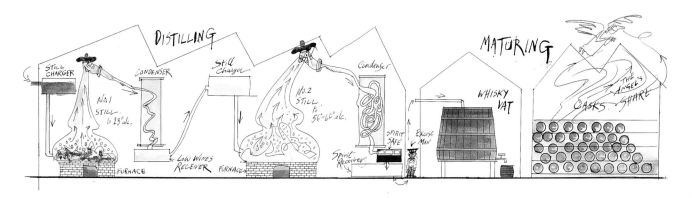

called a worm. The liquid, at this stage, is referred to as low wines. There are other types of condenser using parallel multi-pipes, but distillers still refer to it as the worm. *YOU can use an electric kettle, attaching central heating copper piping with solder to the spout – ask a plumber to do this work if you are not up to it, and he will coil it for you too. Submerge the coil in a sink or similar container of cold water, making use of gravity. Place another receptacle beneath the pipe to catch the low wines. Boil the kettle until dry. Pour it back into the kettle and boil it again but read on below first for technical procedure.*

The second distillation is a little tricky and this is where skill and innate traditional knowledge come into their own.

Only the middle fraction (middle cut) of this distillation is drawn off and passed through the spirit safe, by precise measure, to be stored and matured in casks. At this stage the alcoholic strength is between 53 and 60 degrees of ethanol. Ethanol is still not consid-

ness; it will have mellowed, and it will have absorbed the colour and some of the flavour from the oloroso sherry-soaked casks.

A percentage of the spirit will have evaporated during this time, and although this will pain a true Scotsman – not unreasonably – he philosophically refers to this loss as the angels' share. *YOU must be prepared to react in the same way, and while you are in jail, the result of your efforts can gently mature in some other dark, cool corner you may call your own, for a celebration on your release. How rich and mellow your particular distillation will turn out to be will depend on your cunning, native expertise, as much as the length of time you are inside. Five years, 10 years, 15, 25. That all depends on the judge and his particular preference. Judge Angus MacKnockaddu of Claplochshot Brae, for instance, liked a wee dram of 25 year-old straight from the cask after a trial. He is a hard but honourable man and if he can wait 25 years for a wee dram of your hard stuff, so can you, Aye!*

N
PULTENEY
CLYNELISH
DINGWALL
INVERNESS
SKYE
TALISKER
CULLODEN
HIGHLANDS
GLEN GARIOCH
ABERDEEN
OBAN
MULL
PERTH
THE BORDER
DUNDEE
EDINBURGH
GLENKINCHIE
JURA
ISLAY
GLASGOW
ARRAN
CAMPBELLTOWN
LOWLAND
NOTHIN'
SPRINGBANK
Mull of KINTYRE
BLADNOCH
CARLISLE
MONARCH of the GLEN

Islay

Islay malts are known particularly for their peatiness, and a strong salt-sprayed, aye, aye, Cap'n, seaweedy flavour; they are the most pungent of all whiskies. Islay remains a self-contained powerhouse of distinction and I will eulogise upon the subject strictly on request.

The Regions

Campbeltown

Campbeltown is on a large substantial peninsula, enclosing the Isle of Arran and protecting it in a way that suggests something rather manly and virile. It is no accident that the church bell in Campbeltown is blessed with a loud dong. There is nothing camp about that bell. The pun is irresistible and so is the whisky – strong-bodied, pulsating warmth and a salty tang of smugglers' caves. Nowadays, only two distilleries, Glen Scotia and Springbank, are in action out of the 33 that flourished in the vaporous days of mid-19th century optimism. By the time Alfred Barnard visited, in 1885, 20 were going strong and they continued to do so until World War I. Some were mothballed, then reopened, only to be withered by American Prohibition in the 1920s.

Lowlands

Lowland whiskies are lighter, with a sweeter quality. But some, like Auchentoshan, are triple-distilled, light, but intense and nutty, rather like one of those geldings in fettle again! They get leaner and less sweet with age, but who doesn't? For a whisky, it is a bonus.

Highlands

Highland malts are the spoiled brats of whiskies, which only means that they have got it all – eagles, red deer, grouse, heather moors, lochs, glens, mountain peaks and wildest abandon.

Smoky, rather than peaty, they exude a kind of Scottish pride and wealth, which is considered sophisticated. In many ways it is, but, to an outsider, it can also be interpreted as an over-exercised national pride and smugness which, thankfully, are absent from the Highlands' superlative art of whisky-making. The Highlanders are generous and ingenious enough to make sure that only that which is breathtaking and lifegiving about their environment is put inside a handy bottle, with a hint of sweetness to help it on its way to softening the stoniest heart. (My editor is a Scotsman, and he appreciates the poetic bits.)

The Speyside single malts, along the river Spey, are especially favoured by blenders to balance their blends because of the sublety of the style. Nothing is too pronounced, except the concentration of fine distilleries in this region. Further east there is a thinning-out of distilleries and a more varied style and quality which perhaps discourages all but the most daring blenders, bearing in mind that consistency is the yardstick and even a restraining conservatism – but that is only my triple-distilled opinion.

Orkney

The Orkney Islands are a Nordic law unto themselves, and the stronghold of one of the finest malts it has ever been my privilege to watch in production and to taste in profusion – Highland Park.

GLEN TURRET

Ralph (speaking into tape recorder): I'm up above the distillery of Glenturret, looking round at the most wonderful vist – aaaaaarrrggghhhh!!! shit!!! and I'm surrounded by oh bugger it, it's all over my shoes, rabbit warrens and hundreds of rabbits all dropping everyth – sod it! – running about all over the place – my foot! I can't move my foot!! John call the emergenc – what? can't hear – goddamnit – never mind – aaaarrrrrggggghhhh!!!! OK – clambering out – moving to different places as I move along and I'm on a sort of slopeaaaarrrggggghhh, shit, sod it, a little bit dodgy but otherwise it's all right – OK, no problem

I can unfortunately only see the Pagoda Restaurant – bloody awful food – what can you expect from Scaaarrrggghhhtish barbarians – raaaaarrrrgggghhhh!! liver? – I can't quite see round the corner to the old distillery itself. There it is! Yes!! – and there's one of the buildings still here – there – which has been turned into a baaaarrrggggghhhhh!!! and restaurant heaving with tourism. But I can hear the river from here. I can just see it amongst the trees, a beautiful brown waaaarrrggghhhhtteeerrr, shit!, clear as a bell – but with that tinge of brown, a peaty – look out!! . . .

Royal BRACKLA

A distillery I had never heard of, but which now stands out in my mind as a particularly distinctive one.

Standing inside the still room, which houses four stills, I looked out at what is perhaps the most convenient juxtaposition I have ever seen. To my left, are the old bonded warehouses. Centrally placed are the three reservoirs constantly refilled by the Cawdor Burn, where all the water for distilling Royal Brackla is drawn. There is an underground water supply, which is now used exclusively to cool the swirling spirit vapours which rise like Palamino horses from the stills. To my right, and immediately alongside Cawdor Burn Reservoir, is the barley field. What immaculate planning!

Unfortunately, this rare single malt is only available at the distillery itself, or from selected distributors in the Lowlands. This was a tradition started by the founder, Captain William Fraser of Brackla House. He became a licensed distiller, early in the 19th century, but found it very difficult to compete with the illicit stills, who paid nothing to nobody and didn't intend to. This did not seem fair to him and he reported his plight to a Parliamentary Commission in 1821. He had sold less than 100 gallons for immediate consumption within a radius of 120 miles in a year, and yet, inhabitants for miles around drank whisky, and only whisky, like Coca Cola.

Hence the development of a distribution network in the Lowlands and an advertising campaign, plus King William IV's blessing. He commanded a regular supply at his royal chambers from 1835, in the thieving tradition of royal personages.

It seems that between 1827 and 1844 Captain Fraser got into a spot of trouble with H.M. Customs and Excise. I suspect that His Majesty became a useful ally at that time and, in exchange for overlooking certain discrepancies, earned the Captain's devotion.

It became known as 'The King's Own Whisky' and Captain Fraser mended his ways. Hence the prefix 'Royal' to the name Brackla.

Royal BRACKLA Distillery - THE VIEW.

Royal Brackla prospered with the blessing of the new Excise Act of 1823, which eased restrictions on those who went legal. It earned the title 'The Drink Divine', and Queen Victoria gave it a Royal Warrant of Appointment in 1838.

The House of Andrew Usher & Co. of Edinburgh became Royal Brackla's agents until the turn of the century. It was the Ushers who introduced the art of blending in the 1860s and, together with the Frasers, created proprietary blends, probably some of the first of their kind offered to the public.

Brackla was the stiff drink favoured by explorers seeking the source of the Nile in the 1860s and is eulogised in diaries and letters of the period. 'My dear Fanny, I am bearing up. The river is longer than I imagined. The tigers can be a trifle bothersome but I bag them when I can. The worst are the mosquitoes which can only be held at bay when my blood is pulsating with a goodly snort of Brackla'.

All the distilleries of Islay are built next to the sea. In the old days when the small ships had to come in, there was no point in having a distillery ten miles inland. It had to get to Scotland. On a really stormy day, the sea's over that wall. That gate we just drove in, I've seen barrels floating out that gate. Empty ones!

Jim McEwan, Bowmore distillery

15

PEAT

Cutting peat is perhaps one of the less common pursuits of ordinary folk and, I would imagine, is practically non-existent among the aristocracy, though I heard a whisper that the occasional Irish lord would take his turn, between hangovers, to clear the head. Peat bogs are invariably windswept and, in that way, perfectly situated for the purpose for which they were cut, which was generally to keep a body warm. Basically, peat is cut as a fuel which, being dense in texture in its waterlogged state, is extracted from straight-cut peat-banks and left to dry in long 18 inch by 5 inch square blocks in wigwam-style piles called fixings. When dry, it is black and hard and, in some cases, not unlike coal.

Cutting peat is not an unpleasant experi-ence, if you only have a yard or so to deal with. If you are a serious peat cutter with a real purpose then you purchase about 80 yards of peat bog, about a yard wide, and you cut 18 inch-deep furrows. First, cut off the top 8 inches of grass-covered peat before removing your particular area. This amount will keep a fire going for an average heavy Scottish winter, and fill your house with the most delicious, aromatic and musty smell you can imagine.

The tools used to cut this fuel supply con-

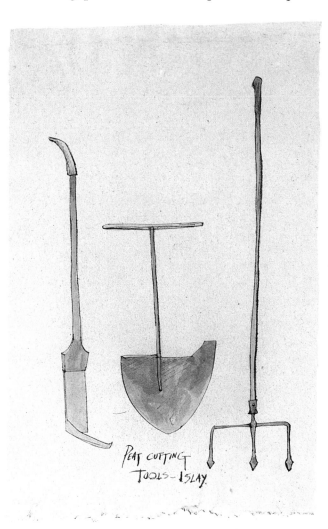

PEAT CUTTING
TOOLS—ISLAY

PEAT
CUTTERS and
GOLDEN EAGLE

sist of a flat shovel to remove the top layer; then a right-angled cutting tool with a cranked horn-bone handle on the holding-end, to control the direction of the cut. This enables you to cut directly downwards, but at a slight angle, so that the soft cheeselike piece can be lifted out all within the same motion and laid on the grass-covered bank at your side. The third tool is a three-pronged fork for lifting out fallen pieces, whole or broken, to be laid neatly side-by-side with the rest. A peatcutter refreshes his parts with a mixture of water and oats – uncooked porridge in fact. It quenches your thirst like nothing else.

Deeper channels are cut periodically, to allow water to drain away, particularly from areas where you are working, otherwise flooding would result and work would be impossible. Attention is given to the depth of cut in one area to control the overall regularity so that, at a later date, another layer can be extracted with as much ease and uniformity as the cut before.

There is also a machine for peat cutting

which is regrettably rather like open cast mining. An area is literally chain-sawed out by a 4-inch wide chain saw of scoops which drives the peat into a compressor and out through a series of fanned tubes like spaghetti. These are allowed to dry in the sun and wind before being collected by a harvester conveyor-belt which throws the turd-shaped pieces into a truck moving alongside the tractor. All vehicles have at least three tyres per wheel to minimise the sinking of the heavy machinery into the sponge-like peat which reacts like a waterbed underfoot.

When you cut three feet down with a peat chain saw and gouge out the under matter, what fills it up? Is it water? Does it create a waterlogged substrata? Professor Brad Quatako of Ottawa Institute of Advanced Peataqua Studies at the University of Algonquin says, 'Yes, and worse, air too, which turns foul when trapped. It causes embarrassing histrionic effects when trodden on. It could mean the end of romance for the peat dwellers.'

I suspect that with continuous moving pressure of this intensity, the time-formed nature of the oily substance breaks down and its inherent qualities are impaired, if not damaged forever.

How environmentally friendly this mechanised invasion is will only be revealed in time. It is the subject of much debate, and various pressure groups have voiced many objections to its practice, particularly against its use in the malting of barley where it is burned in furnaces topped by pagoda-shaped drying attics. It is this drying and smoking process which imparts to whisky, especially Islay whisky, its seaweedy pungent flavour, the 'medicinal' characteristic of Islay single malts. Two thirds of the burning goes up in CO_2 – but oxygen is created. Nothing is wasted, I can vouch for that, and whisky distilling is still one of the most effectively environmentally friendly industries. Even the boiled barley mash is recycled as cattle fodder called draff.

It seemed like a good idea at the time, but nothing is replaced. Peat cannot be replaced

Ralph Steadman '91   Derelict Croft & Peat Furrows, Islay – 2 Sept 91.

PEAT STACK 1

PEAT STACK TOO

PEAT CUTTING

In those days the men used to get five or six drams and the old boys preferred it straight from the still – white spirit. In the summer time we had a problem because there was no white spirit being produced, so the manager would say to me, 'Go and draw us a really good dram for the lads at five o'clock. Choose the best dram.' The really old worthies would come in and say it wasn't strong enough! They liked a really good hit. It all stopped in 1978.

Jim McEwan, Bowmore distillery

Below: Machined peat

any more than coal can. The increased demand for the raw material of the land imposes a pressure that had never existed before. The industrialised peat cutting can only disturb an environmental balance that was maintained in earlier times. The local needs were in rhythm with the available resources. The peat was cut for basic heating and a much smaller whisky output. The top soil was replaced and the land resumed its natural course. Its wildlife was hardly damaged, merely disturbed temporarily. Now vast tracts of peat bog lie like open wounds, and the mechanical disturbance, even the massive weight of its bulk, compressing the ground in such an unprecedented fashion, is reminiscent of the despoliation of forests to make way for new roads – a despoliation from which the land never recovers. No one can really say whether such policies are good or bad ones, since they have never been tried before. Mechanical peat cutting appears to show the same propensity for damage, as other forms of exploitation, in other industries. While it may certainly be easier on the back, and a machine can do the work of a hundred men in a fraction of the time, what price the future if unseen cycles of nature's regenerative forces cause other bio-systems to live or die?

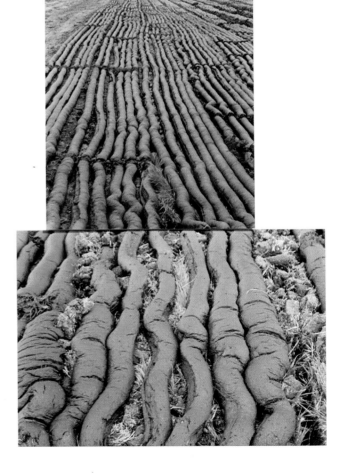

GLENROTHES DISTILLERY — SPEYSIDE

GLENROTHES DISTILLERY CATHEDRAL, SPEYSIDE.

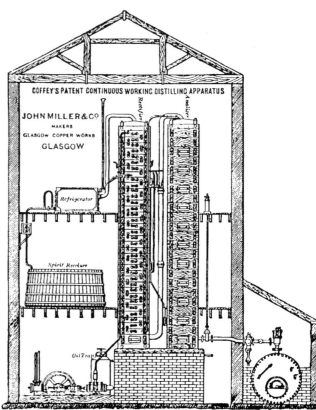

Above: Forsythe's Still-yard, Rothes

Ralph STEADMAN 9/3

Patent STILL

The patent still revolutionised whisky-making. It was originally invented by Richard Stein, in 1826, but was perfected by Aeneas Coffey in the 1850s which has established him as its inventor. Grain was used in a continuous process which speeded up the production of basic industrial spirit and hastened in the science of blending various distilled liquors with pure single malts from the various regions of Scotland. Independent of geographic location, it created an outrage and to some became a mockery of the traditional drink familiar to Scotsmen everywhere. It seemed to strike at the very heart of stills of illicit magnificence.

Copper Stills and Mash

It has to be copper – only copper will do. Copper is soft and copper is clean – come and get me, copper! A cut from copper will heal about a week earlier than it does if you cut yourself on steel. Try it. Copper is beaten and steel is rolled, and copper is fashioned by machine into more regular shapes like mash-tuns, washbacks and fermentation tanks with straight sides.

Coppersmiths always made pot stills by hand. They had to and they still do, but they do other things to survive in our rapidly changing world of virtual reality. Rarely does a new distillery open, and those in existence require a new still but it is only a once-in-a-lifetime occurrence. But stills do need repairs. Some parts of a still wear out quicker than others, so repair work is a fairly constant necessity. A visit to Forsyth's in Rothes is a visit to a metalwork factory of great diversity.

The heads and swan necks of a pot still go first, after about 10 to 12 years, because of the corrosive effect of the low wine vapours (the first distillation) on the metal. The bulging part, the pot, will last 20 to 25 years, maybe more. Then the bottom will go on a direct-fire still, where the heat, at anything between 600 and 700 degrees centigrade, is in direct contact with the thicker copper bottom. The indirectly heated pot stills have thinner copper bottoms, but will last longer. They have an internal, tubular, stainless steel heating ring, rather like an electric kettle, with added fancy cylindrical augmenters to increase the heating surface and distribute the heat more efficiently inside the pot. Condensers, the cooling part of the distillation process, will last about 25 years, but they too may develop faults at different times in their labyrinth of copper tubing, inside the main cold water trunk, which is also made of copper.

Ancient Stills, Strathisla
(Heart of Chivas Regal) (circa 1786)
Ralph Steadman

All that has changed over 200-odd years are the welding techniques, but the joints are still hand-hammered into shape. Because they taper and curve in so many directions, each section will be made from three or four smaller sections.

Some pot stills have a swelling at the base of the neck like a huge goiter, called a boilball, or Ogee in Greek, which is meant to compensate for reflux. Reflux is the fallback of vapours which don't quite make it over the top of the swan neck and condense backwards, as it were. Reflux is corrosive. In attempts to minimise this effect, necks have been widened, narrowed, squatted, heightened, and boilballed, but the essential alembic shape has never changed. The slight differences and sizes have all evolved out of hunches, constant performance results, habits, and, probably, accidents. Beliefs in some inherent and mystical ability proven by results over generations are peculiar to any and every distillery, including superstition, and dents in the copper that may well be the very thing that singles out one malt from another. The dents are always replaced exactly as they were whenever repairs are made.

Denters, of course, are artists and command great respect and humbling. You can't just make any old dent with a big hammer and walk away. It requires the ear and intuition of a piano tuner to hit the right note, and, if it's not right, a whole panel may have to be made again, at great cost. It could be claimed that a fractional mistake could mar the whole symphony, which after all is what the whisky-making process is. Likewise, you cannot learn denting; you are born with it. Many Scottish households encourage their offspring, hardly out of nappies, by giving them hammers and the kitchen pots and pans, to bang away to their hearts' content in the hope of discovering a born denter in the family. Those who haven't quite got the knack often become drummers in the Argyll Highlanders. But I digress . . .

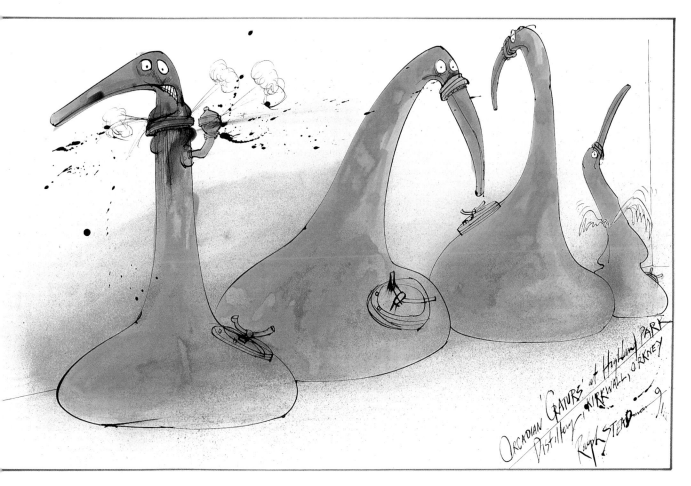

'Orcadian Craturs' at Highland Park Distillery, Kirkwall, Orkney — Ralph STEADman

Glen Ord

Glen Ord has many parts of its 19th-century architecture intact, although the bonded warehouses are renovated. The newer additions sit awkwardly, as though a part of something else. The pot stills stand proudly, however – a row of six copper icons, glowing in the sunlight shining through the window-fronted facade.

That is its most spectacular feature. The rest is functional, bleak and corrugated. Glen Ord's own maltings are colossal, the tallest in Scotland, and dominate the surrounding flat countryside for miles.

COOPERAGE

There was a cooper and his cask, with a hey and a ho and a hey nonny no! . . .

Speyside is the heart of the Scottish malt whisky industry, if only because more of it is produced in this area and with more consistency over a longer period.

It is also central, geographically, and is therefore surrounded by all the rest, even

FIRING A CASK — SPEYSIDE COOPERAGE.

Donny's Inferno

In firing an old cask, the heads are removed from each end and it is placed over a furnace, with a metal plate laid over the top. The heat builds up inside and the wood is, quite literally, toasted. Then the cooper removes the metal plate, allowing the intense heat to burst out. It is removed from the *heat and hosed until it is cool. This process restores the toasty flavours to the wood and over the years, these influence the nature of the whisky. Casks are blistered in the firing and this roughness is left to add to the flavour-imparting properties of the oak. The flames sterilise every tiny crack. Nothing purifies like fire, except whisky itself.*

CROSS SECTION OF TREE SHOWING HOW THE BULK IS PLANKED — THE RINGS SHOULD CROSS THE PLANK AS DIRECTLY AS POSSIBLE TO MINIMISE WARPING.

THE COOPER'S WOOD AND TOOLS

CHIME

HEAD

QUARTER

BOOGE

PITCH

BOOGE

QUARTER

CHIME

DRESSED STAVE

STAVE SHAPING

TOPPING PLANE

HEADING VICE

INSIDE SHAVE

DOWNRIGHT

HOOP PUNCH

COOPER'S BLOCK and BLOCK HOOK

A CHIV

AUGER

BOW SAW

BARREL HEAD SECTION SHOWING DOWELLED BUTT JOINTS.

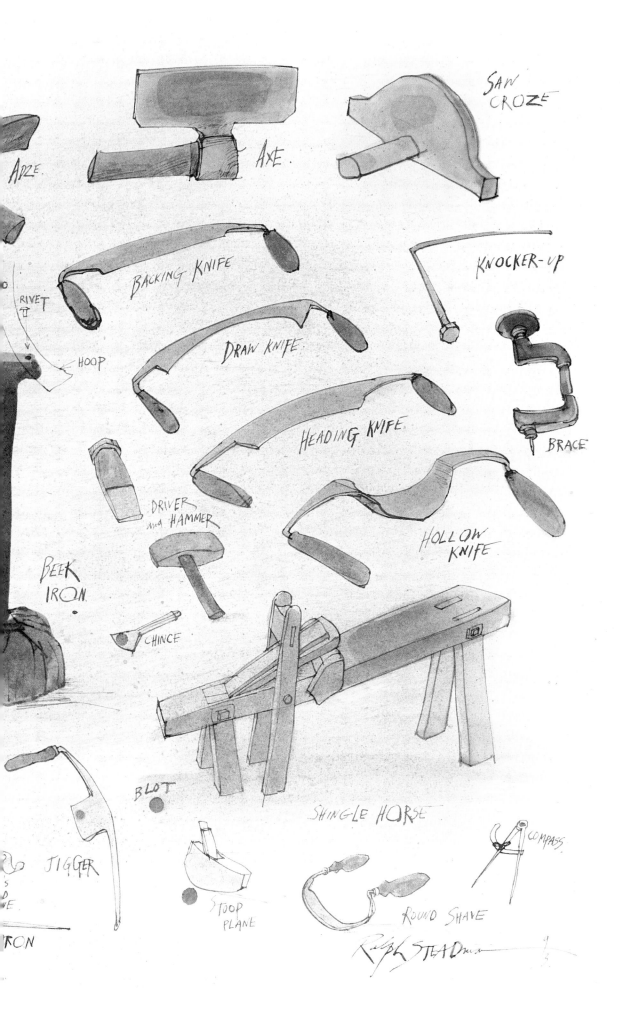

ADZE.

AXE.

SAW CROZE

BACKING KNIFE

KNOCKER-UP

RIVET

HOOP

DRAW KNIFE.

BRACE

HEADING KNIFE

DRIVER and HAMMER

HOLLOW KNIFE

BEEK IRON.

CHINCE

SHINGLE HORSE

BLOT

JIGGER

STOOP PLANE

ROUND SHAVE

COMPASS.

IRON

Ralph STEADman

though much of the rest could be classed as central too. Scotland is full of centres of the finest, the purest, and the best of single malts, each with a distinctive claim as fervently believed in as the others, and each one central and peculiar to itself. One thing, however, these centres all have in common – the cask. In this, ethanol spirit, from every region, is matured for the minimum three years before it can claim the right to call itself whisky.

The Egyptians made straight-sided, segmented, wooden vessels, held firm with wooden hoops, 3,000 years before Christ. In Greek, Roman and Phoenician civilisations and their enclaves around the Mediterranean, terracotta clay vessels were preferred well into the first few centuries AD, though some underwater excavations have revealed barrels with hoops made from tied willow, and with the bent stave pattern. Paradoxically, coopering established itself in this part of Europe where trees are, in fact, sparse. The craft spread north, west and east where much of the best wood, from slow-growing dense forests, was to be found. The denseness, incidentally, encourages tall, straight trunks with the minimum of knots. There are over 50 species of oak tree worldwide, each species with qualities and natural tannins of its own,

THE EGYPTIAN INFLUENCE — CASK STACKING at SPEYSIDE COOPERAGE.

which interact and impart a flavour to the contents of a cooper's cask. The Romans called these casks *cupals* and their maker a *cuparius*.

The making of casks has changed little since Roman times and neither have the tools, which retain the look of ancient, but practical simplicity; only now, they are not made of stone or bronze.

Only a few oak species are favoured to fulfil all cooperage essentials – strong, tight, regular grain being the most important for ease of working. Of oak used today in Scotland 97% comes from North America (from the north-facing slopes of the Appalachian mountains, Missouri, Kentucky and Tennessee), the white oak, *Quercus Alba*, being the favourite for the light, elegant flavour it imparts to a delicate malt. Some distilleries prefer to age whisky in old casks already impregnated with oloroso sherry, for a richer, spicy, dark finish. Sessile oak from North-west Spain is richer and more robust in flavour, as is Memel oak from Eastern Europe. Limousin oak from France is also a cooper's favourite but is used mainly for the maturation of wines. The Egyptians, incidentally, lined their barrels with tar to prevent the wood from tainting their wines, and to seal the wood.

While oak is, like all woods, porous, it resists seepage but does enable the contents to breathe.

Logs are 'quarter sawn' (see clever drawing on previous page) so that at least one dense medullary ray appears in the length and the breadth of each stave when cut to size. A medullary ray is the ring of slower winter growth that creates denser, narrow bands of cells in circles through a cross-section in the trunk. These tighter cells also resist warping. Several years of seasoning are crucial before use.

The coopers repairing old casks at the Speyside Cooperage in Craigellachie, Aberlour, in Banffshire, demonstrate to a kind of glass-enclosed spectator-balcony a labour-intensive craft, brutally hard work, minimised only by the sheer ability of the cooper and his confidence in his skills, learned over a seven-year apprenticeship. Hammering is

incessant and the noise ear-shattering. Soundproofed ear-muffs are advisedly worn in the workshop itself, though some seem not to bother and are perhaps already deaf. The oldest cooper looked little more than 50 and the youngest no more than a lad. They all hammer like demons, removing old hoops called booges, quarters and chimes, and replacing them after a cask has been dismantled, damaged staves replaced, chopped with an adze, shaved with a draw knife and generally re-aligned for a perfect face-up along the edges of each stave. No extra filler should be necessary and natural, damp wood-swell will suffice to eliminate the slightest hairline crack. The conditions of sale are that the customer, the distiller, will be supplied with casks in a condition fit to fill.

A cask is not fitted together – it is 'raised up', a rather biblical phrase, I thought. At this point it looks like a wooden skirt and is ready to be fired, i.e. re-charred (see page 27).

This intensive care of a cask is reflected in its life-span of up to 60 years.

American oak barrels are often imported into the UK after having been used to mature Bourbon for up to eight years. These are 'knocked down', i.e. re-made into larger 'hogsheads' (which hold 250 litres) and sold on to store grain whisky. On a good day the cooperage can restore 400 casks to working condition again, at around £70–£90 a time. A new cask varies in price according to supply and demand but certainly costs £120 and upwards.

Shavings from refurbished casks and casks beyond repair are passed on to a salmon smoke house to end their life as fuel to smoke salmon from Scottish rivers. Some casks are put out to grass as garden tubs. Not such a pathetic end for a worthy and vital part of the Scottish whisky industry. You may sit in the dying light of evening, inside the one half, with a glass in hand looking through orange and purple splashes of everlasting pansies inside the other half, and toast the coopers whose craft lives on.

BOWMORE and BOWMORE Distillery. ISLAY.

BOWMORE

The island of Islay is a mere 25 miles long by 20 miles wide. However, its 7 distilleries and 4,000 inhabitants create between them 150 million pounds of duty for the British Government, from the island's main export of single malt whisky.

The islanders are a proud but modest people, and could afford to pull up the ladder and let the rest of the world go by, if they chose. Instead, they welcome all-comers to share and enjoy their way of life, with a generosity common to people who trust in the basic goodness of others.

Bowmore, the town that gives its name to one of Islay's favourite creations, Bowmore malt whisky, is more or less a steep High Street, swooping down to the harbour from a round church at the top of the hill which has no dark corners or black holes for the Devil to hide in. Instead, the Devil hides in the distillery at the bottom of the hill, overlooking a sea which can be as rough as Scottish kneecaps, and as smooth as the whisky and the glass into which it is poured.

Bowmore is a gentle, peaty single malt, aged in oak, behind walls pounded by sea waters, driven into the bay of Loch Indaal when the Atlantic Ocean breathes itself over the land, and stretches its arms.

The cellars of Bowmore lie below sea level, and the sea's assault imparts a hint of ozone to the maturing, time-blessed nectar, lying still and mysterious in the dark. Absorbing the sea's energy, it stores it up, giving some to the angels and biding its time until the gods call out for theirs.

From a boat the building stands possessively on its own turf, where it has stood for 200 years. Its two pagoda-style peat kilns tower like fairy-tale spires, dispersing the

High St & Parish Church
BOWMORE, ISLAY. 3. Sept 91.

rich, pungent aroma of burning peat up the flared nostrils of God Himself who sighs a satisfied breeze across the land.

Not so the Devil, who lurks and smoulders in the salt-saturated darkness beneath the still house, cursing the spirit safe and its carefully controlled and protected waterfall of duty-bound treasure, pouring endlessly into the spirit receiver, and thence into heavily protected warehouse vats. From there it is dispensed into manageable casks and then sealed with a wooden bung, virtually to remain so for at least 3 years, maybe 5, maybe 10, 15, 21 and even 30 for a specially chosen batch.

The angels wait, like patient clouds on a gentle breeze, to receive their share. God, too, will be blessed with a harvest's hope, but no mention is made of the Devil. It drives him wild with rage and, as he foams, the sea pounds the cellar walls outside, casting empty barrels, like missiles assaulting this bastion, in an attempt to break through its mighty walls and devour the precious contents within.

But on occasions the Devil wins out, though not so much nowadays. Human nature became the Devil's work-horse, and many cunning ways were devised by distillery workers to extract an illicit share, something for nothing, or perhaps a little extra recompense for a job well done. If you stand for any length of time and watch the steady flow of colourless liquid pouring so freely into generous goblets, encased securely in their shining sarcophagus, the spirit safe, the mind wanders and gets to thinking that only the thickness of toughened glass stands between you and it. 'Where can it all go?' you ask yourself; 'Who shall profit?' And how could the most observant and scrupulous authority account for every last drop?

The fact is that they cannot, but they, nevertheless, try, just as those who ponder this

Bowmore Distillery – late evening 3. Sept 91.   Ralph Steadman 91.

bountiful cascade also try, to extract just enough so as not to be noticed. It adds interest to an otherwise monotonous process which is as predictable as it is precious and as easy as ABC . . .

With cunning ingenuity the Customs and Excise realised that the only way that they could prevent a distillery from cheating on this abundance was simply to make the distilleries responsible not only for the production, but also for its impeccable control. The distillers are the only ones who could possibly provide the 24-hour surveillance necessary to ensure this total security. A deal was therefore concluded with the distillers, that they would become the gaugers of their own issue and, consequently, the guardians of their own future well-being. To renege would simply be the end of the distillery. Occasional checks are made on measuring equipment and output, but the basic honesty and survival instincts of distillery managers guarantee a watertight solution, even though the Devil may still curse. The spirit is kept bonded in warehouses, duty-free, but every drop is measured and accounted for, *even the angel's share*. Perhaps that is why the Devil is never mentioned in a distillery. To name him is to invoke him. So they let him hide and they let him curse, and they blind him with light every time they unlock and open the heavy doors that keep him trapped inside . . .

Malting. Stoic Scottish islanders will plough dampened barley for at least a week, day and night, to ensure even germination before peat-smoke drying.

Malting

another 2000 gallons of PURE MALT WHISKY — Ralph Steadman

The malting process is so old. They've been doing this for 200 years, obviously spread out on a cave floor. It's probably a fluke, like everything else. A man was probably storing his barley in a cave and it was so wet it started to shoot and he said, 'I'd better start drying this out and maybe use it.' And when he did dry it out, he found he got better whisky from it. It must have been an accident. He probably had sacks of barley and the rain was pouring down and it got wet and instead of seeing this and, being a Scotsman, being really miserable, he said, 'I don't want to waste it, I'll try to dry it. He was stubborn.'

Jim McEwan, Bowmore distillery

JURA

Sitting here in the quiet, still air with the odd noises of activity, the local bus backing up with its funny little siren, the throbbing sound of a boat, the coast guard launch, entering the harbour, the Paps going slightly dim and becoming sharp again as the mists lift and fall in the sunshine which bathes us all in its mellow, satisfied gentle sway. The fishermen have just come back in their little tug boat, for all the world like a little Pop-eye boat, and delivered lobsters in a basket onto the jetty – obviously the speciality of Port Askaig Hotel. Overlooking the little harbour, Port Askaig Stores and Post Office, established in 1767, sells petrol and oil, and general stores, and is probably a meeting place during the odd morning shop. There are very few tourists but a sufficient, steady little flow of people who have discovered such a place

as this. Sitting inside the harbour wall are two old boats – to some, an eye-sore, to others, a symbol of bravery in the last war. The old CN 82 with its barnacled, moss-dripping hull which was used to ferry men from Dunkirk and is considered to be a symbol of bravery in this region of the islands. The hotelier is not very happy having it there but the owner of the boat said that if it's good enough for carrying Dunkirk survivors back to Scotland, it's good enough to sit in a harbour as a symbol, so there it stays. And what else? The sounds of wheeling, squawking birds, hammering, knocking, people doing things all the time, not very big things, done in a certain slow, rhythmic way. The bus is off out of Port Askaig, probably back to Port Ellen, up and down the island. The island has very few roads; the main road circles it, but is

not completed. The top, northern edge doesn't have a road, maybe just a dirt track. The ferry is now back until the next trip across the Sound of Islay to Jura at three o'clock. It seems to go once every two hours and is only large enough to take six cars at the most, a truck, plus a few foot passengers. It chugs its way back and forth, the journey takes between five and ten minutes and the island of Jura is near enough for us to make it out quite clearly, the shore on the other side and the landscape.

And, of course, the excise officers were the guys who had reached the end of the road, who weren't being promoted. Imagine being consigned to Glen Whatever in 1900 – it was a fate worse than death, really. But there was a mutual trust, in a way. If an excise officer decided to make life difficult for a distillery, the distiller could make life hell for the excise man because within the Excise Act the officer couldn't interfere with production. So if the distillery manager said, 'Right, I want to take charge at four o'clock in the morning,' the excise man had to be there to oversee it, because everything had to be written down. So there was a sort of balance. What's more, the manager didn't even have to be there. He could get one of his subordinates to take charge and he could stay in bed.

Anon

There were a couple of excise officers and one of the things they had to do was take a 'regular' sample of mature whisky so that they could test their instruments. The only way they could do this was to go into the warehouse, draw some mature whisky, get up to their office – they couldn't do it anywhere else – and test their working instruments against the standard instruments. In theory, that stuff was supposed to go back into the cask, but believe me, that equipment was tested to destruction.

Anon

A FAMOUS GROUSE in FULL AUTUMN PLUMAGE with apologies to my friend John HUGHES of MATHEW GLOAG

BLEND..ING

'To say that blending whisky is just a matter of mixing together a few varieties of single malts and grain whiskies, according to a known recipe, to produce a consistent and well-known product with a standard trade name, would be to diminish the art of a blender to nothing more than a pie-maker.' The great 19th-century haggis- and pie-maker Simon Ferintosh McWall said that. Above his baking ovens he had built his own set of stills, ten in all, which worked every time he baked bread. He had the yeast, the know-how, the contacts *and* his own network of smugglers. He made malt bread, of course, and always had surplus supplies which were steeped, germinated and then dried under cover of his legitimate business. Shipments of illicit whisky were hidden beneath tons of his venison pies and indeed their own piecrust. It always reached the Lowlands undetected. Suspicions were only roused when he was once interrupted nose-ing one of his own pies during a visit from a Weights and Measures inspector. He absent-mindedly referred to it as a fine wee dram. He

The BLENDER NOSEING.

Quality CONTROL: Everything is tasted and analysed. The slightest impurity is a failure. 100% is the only standard.

became famous as the Dingwall Jail baker and then the Jailbreaker – 'a file with every pie', but I digress . . .

A blender is a man with rare powers of scent – a bloodhound of sorts who can detect the slightest foreign body and then eliminate it. His goal is to ensure that the blend of a high-quality whisky is precisely the same in each and every bottle, given that variables will inevitably occur and must be compensated for by the addition of a nuance of another distiller's spirit. The balance must be as near as a nose hair to the inherent qualities that the imbiber has come to expect from his whisky . . .

The variables are practically infinite, no matter how careful, scrupulous and exacting each individual distiller is, and they are all of that. Quality reigns supreme throughout the industry. However, nature being the heartland of all processes, changes are inevitable. Atmosphere, temperatures, humidity, water temperatures, barley, the judgement of the still manager and the workers whose task it is to know when each process is complete – all affect the final spirit. Slight changes are inevitable, but these changes are not generally defects – just differences, undetectable to the average person. However, to a blender they are a signal to adjust the blend, to compensate and, therefore, achieve the recognised consistency. The operation is about as difficult as remembering everybody's face in the crowd at Murrayfield, but a blender practically has that astonishing ability. I say practically, because several blenders work together and ask each other if something is suspect. I would place them at the very pinnacle of the art of whisky-making and nominate them the true experts in a complex world of contradiction and personal opinions.

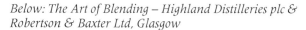

You have to tune in – at first you're not that sharp. Sometimes you can pick it up, odours come off and if you don't catch them early on you sometimes miss them. I don't drink a lot of whisky.

Whisky Blender

Below: The Art of Blending – Highland Distilleries plc & Robertson & Baxter Ltd, Glasgow

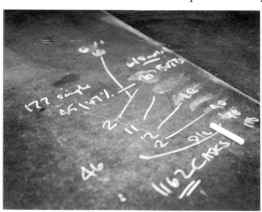

Highland Park

Highland Park is a kind of St Peter's Gate to its town of Kirkwall on the Orkney's, and lord of all it surveys.

Orkney's remoteness from the mainstream of whisky production enhances its sense of uniqueness. There is only one other distillery on the island – Scapa (named after the concrete-blocked Scapa Flow of World War II fame), which, I suspect, lacks nothing but investment in its ability to produce a single malt as concrete as anything that the island is famous for, including the standing stones at the Ring of Brogar, and the 5,000 year-old settlement at Skara Brae. There is a wisp of highland heather in the peatreek smoky blue flavours captured inside the pagoda-shaped bottle of Highland Park, which should just as well apply to a Scapa dram.

(The proprietor of THE SHOP in Kirkwall, purveyors of fish and foodstuffs to Her Majesty the Queen, was more than in agreement with my poetic assessment as I purchased his own brand of peaty haggis which exploded in the baggage hold on our return flight via Aberdeen. I found a suitable replacement at Martin's of George Street in Aberdeen, a tip for those who go haggis-hunting when in the neighbourhood.)

HIGHLAND PARK Distillery — approaching — KIRKWALL, ORKNEY   Ralph STEADman

SCAPA

In fact, a bottle of Scapa turned up at Heathrow airport, where we were on our way to Lyon to make a pilgrimage to Burgundy country. Scapa 10 year-old single malt is a fine dram, a flawless echoed dream of lapping waves against the peated, rocky beaches of the Lingro Burn from whence it came, resonating in some foreign clime like a reassuring friend, and no more so than in the damp country air of Brouillard just outside Beaune. Here, in the Hostellerie du Vieux Moulin, which my editor, who was in the same jam as me, renamed the Hostility of Mutton dressed as Lamb, the honest, salty strength of the Scapa kept us honour-bound to hold our blunder on course and suffer yet another three nights in that Nouvelle Amex bunker, which managed to lose another Michelin star as we tried to figure out whether the chef wanted to satisfy our raging hunger or teach us quantum physics with wafer-thin sliced carrots and radiating spirals of mangetout peas. Scapa replaced the Knockando (my choice from some promotion-pushy honker in the duty-free shop), but later made a rather interesting blend. Adding the bourbon sweetness of the Knockando forged a strange and evocative marriage which lent another dimension to the Scapa, but would probably make an Orcadian emigrate to Greenland and weep blocks of ice. Nevertheless it broke our shackles, strengthened our resolve – and with one mighty leap we were free!

The Queen was here in 1980 – that's the Queen's barrel there. It's been maturing since then and we've informed the keeper of the royal cellar. I would think they'll take the barrel. It will be interesting to find out if they are going to charge the Queen any duty on it.

Jim McEwan, Bowmore distillery

STRATHISLA Distillery – Keith, Banffshire.

ARDBEG Distillery . ISLAY.

Lagavulin Distillery, ISLAY (home of WHITE HORSE) (and a SMUGGLER'S HAUNT) Ralph STEADman 91

LAPHROAIG →

Of the survivors from the 1745 Jacobite Rebellion, three brothers – the Johnstons of the Clan MacIan (MacDonald), from Ardnamurchan, left the mainland and arrived in Islay to find work. They all became farmers and distilled their own whisky – a practice more common on Islay than anywhere else in Scotland. The sons of one brother settled at Laphroaig and started a small distillery about 1812. One was diligent and went legal in 1826 and had bought the other out by 1836, remaining a tenant on land owned by the Campbells.

He died by what could be described as a brewer's death of the thousand gulps. He fell into a vat of burnt ale and lived only two days after, but he did set the record for the longest pee in history. He left a second wife and six children, two of them sons who were far too young to run a distillery. The business was leased to another distillery, Lagavulin, just a couple of hundred yards down the road, until Dugald, the youngest son, became old

enough to take over, which he did in 1857, with the guidance of Lagavulin. They remained his agents until 1907, though Dugald himself had already gone to the great distiller in the sky in 1877. He left no heirs.

Now, I appreciate that this is a bit of a saga so you'll have to concentrate. *His* sister Isabella, right?, had married *his* brother Alexander Johnston of Tallant (whoops! though I might be mistaken) who ran the distillery for his wife, and *her* other three sisters who had a share in the business. OK? Now, Isabella died and husband Alexander inherited *her* share, but *he* died too in 1907, leaving a hell of a legal mess behind. This was the stuff of TV soap dramas. Court case followed court case. *Two* of the three sisters were finally awarded ownership but one of them had married a William Hunter. *He* had a nephew, a Glasgow tram engineer called J. Johnston Hunter, who *also* now got a piece of the action.

However, it was Mrs William Hunter's son, Ian, who after finishing his training as an engineer on the mainland, hastily returned to Islay in 1908 and controlled the business on behalf of his mother and *her* sister, *his*

Aunt Katherine. The distillery appears to have flourished between 1877 and the turn of the century and much building was done during that time. Then, at the time of Alex Johnston's death in 1907, things seem to have got in a bit of a pickle (and if this had been a TV drama there would have been a murder just about here). Son Ian reckoned that the Mackie family who owned Lagavulin had not been too generous as agents and he broke off business relations with them. After a blazing row Mr Mackie went beserk and got his men to pull out the foundation stones of Laphroaig's water source, effectively cutting it off.

I know from personal experience (and Thomas Hardy!) that some country people do dumb spiteful things like that. I have had access to my own cesspit obstructed for nearly five years now. I do not want to distil its contents of course, but if it is left much longer, we could have a mini Mount Etna lava flow on our hands which could threaten a third of Kent. But I digress . . .

Following another court case, Mr Mackie of Lagavulin had to repair the damage and restore the vital water supply, but not before enticing Laphroaig's master brewer away to make malt whisky for him. (Yet another twist for my TV drama.) The strange thing is, and it *is* the case in many other such situations of close proximity, that even using the same type of pot still *and* the same water, *and* even the same brewer, Mr Mackie could not make the same 'peatreek' whisky – a mere 200 yards away on the same coast. And whilst I am on the subject, neither is Ardbeg whisky the same just 200 yards further on from Laphroaig, in the other direcion. It is still an intriguing mystery today and confounds absolute scientific analysis, though experts harumph amongst themselves that it is merely a matter of natural variants, and so it is, but a mystery of nature nevertheless. In fact, so patently obsessed with maintaining continuity and consistent quality are all individual distillers, that, when they install a new still, they will even have the same dents and peculiarities bashed back into it just in case it is those blemishes which influence a distinctive taste. Now, try and tell me *that* is a scientific procedure, but I digress yet again.

Meanwhile (back in our new TV drama),

Laphroaig Distillery (The beautiful hollow by the broad bay). Ralph Steadman

the court cases nearly broke Laphroaig, but Ian Hunter was a good businessman and bought the land from new owners in 1921, the Ramsays of Kildalton, and from under the very nose of Mr Mackie himself, who even then tried to outbid Ian Hunter. Finally, each of the three distilleries bought their own land and their squabbles settled down to a pleasant bitchy co-existence. Laphroaig increased its production capacity with the help of their new agents, Robertson and Baxter, to double its previous output.

In 1927 Ian Hunter went completely independent and started to sell direct, probably after the death of his other partners, his cousin the tram engineer, in 1922, and his Aunt Katherine in 1927, leaving him and his mother as sole owners. The Johnston Hunters seem to have been quietly giving up the ghost or perhaps taking to the spirit. Families are funny things and only ever really show up when there is a will to be read or a wedding to attend, and, of course, Christmas.

His mother died in 1928 and Ian Hunter ran it entirely alone until 1950 when he became a limited company and made himself Managing Director until his death in 1954 (and that's good for a couple of episodes, and so is the next bit). His secretary, Miss Williamson, became Managing Director and ran the place with the efficiency of a humming bird until it fell into the hands of Long John in 1967. But *she* must have been quite some character, a backroom matriarch perhaps, who guided Ian Hunter's decisions like a Scottish Joan Collins. (In fact in *my* TV drama Miss Williamson takes over Long John, Matthew Gloag *and* United Distillers and sets up her power base on Islay, the Dallas of the Western Isles, eventually becoming Life Grand Mistress of the Keepers of the Quaich and Lady Malt of Jura, because she stayed single all her life. It's a winner and by the time you read this, we will be half way through the production schedule of

September Heather   10 Sheets 200lb / 400 gsm   Ralph Steadman

BIG L – The Saga of Distilled Illicit Passions in the Whisky Business.) In real life, however, Miss Williamson remained Laphroaig's Chairman and Managing Director until she retired in 1972. An intriguing life history of just one distillery, more because of what is left out than what is put in. (There are over 180 others. I could keep the series going for years!)

I once threw a party for the launch of my illustrated version of *Treasure Island* at my local pub in Loose, Kent because I had used the pub as the model for The Admiral Benbow in the book. I remember the slogan for the party. It was 'GET LEGLESS ON LONG JOHN'. I wonder if they remember, because we don't.

LAIRD: Now gentlemen – am I to understand that we intend to drink like gentlemen?
GUEST: Of course, sire, of course!
LAIRD: Good man; then we can get as drunk as farts!

Duty was imposed on spirits unfairly in relation to beer because the brewers were the biggest supporters of the Tory Government. They gave masses of funds to the Government 150 years ago. They were keeping the brewers happy.

Anon

There was an old spirit safe in one distillery which once had a tube welded into it which led to a nearby pub, so that they could take the whisky straight from the spirit safe into the pub and serve it to customers. There is a lot of evidence that this actually happened.

Anthony Troon, Journalist

THE EDRADOUR

3rd February, 1994

A tasting of this distinctive little malt, on the shores of Paphos on the island of Cyprus. It was 5.30 pm local time when we claimed room 352 at the Imperial Beach Hotel. We had travelled most of the day. I looked out across the sea. The sun emerged on the horizon like a fierce red boil, erupting through the purple black flesh of a threatening storm-heavy sky, spread out across a wet blanket of Mediterranean gloom.

'Told you I'd show you a good time', gasped Anna spontaneously. Anna has a way with words and was busy getting her diary started. I needed three things right away – the toilet, ointment for my first ever haemorrhoid, a shower, a walk around our immediate surroundings, a swim in the low-lit indoor pool, a long hot bath to appease my second need and a stiff drink. That's seven needs and that's life, but not a bad opening for a whisky tasting.

At a time like this only The Edradour will do. Edradour is the smallest distillery in Scotland, claiming that the minimum-sized stills, their own (500 gallons per charge) produce the best, most intense and concentrated drop of poetry in the southern Highlands just above Perth. This is not quite true. The best drop of sheer poetry, according to tradition and poetic license, was always produced in a squarer-shaped still of only 41 gallons, 2 pints, and 13 16ths, approximately, secreted in heather-bound hideaways miles from any-where, but who is to know? It's all a pack of personal folk tales and supposition and many a duty-free dram was coaxed from the crudest utensil that never saw the light of legend beyond the luckiest few. Rumour has it that the secretion from the lymph node of a stag in rut, added to an illicit charge in the heat of the moment, transforms an otherwise normal high-quality dram into nothing less than the sweat of excitement refreshed in the baths of Aphrodite. But don't quote me on that. The Scots have an uncanny knack of reducing even a love goddess's Olympian consummations to nothing more than an excuse for scandalous behaviour. Aphrodite was, after all, a blacksmith's wife and in Scotland you can still get married over a blacksmith's anvil in Gretna Green, but not to Aphrodite, merely to the love of your life, some mortal Amazon from your own dream factory. The drink, however, The Edradour, in spite of Scottish pride and an over-indulgent use of Scottish reserve, remains Godlike – a nectar for the aforementioned moment to which I have just alluded – in room 352.

LEDRUM SNITTY, an islander who never lost his ability to snitch on his best mates. He seemed to be able to gain their trust, have them tell all and then shop them. He was from St Kilda in the Outer Hebrides and came to seek his fortune on the mainland. His shifty ways suited him well as a look-out man for the sma' still men. He was granted safe passage by the British for his inside help during the Clearances, when whole communities were forcibly ejected from their crofts to seek whatever fate had in store for them. His knowledge of their ways proved invaluable to the officers in charge of this terrible persecution, and cunning and deceit became his stock in trade. He journeyed east until at last he came to Balblair where illicit distilling activity was intense. His shiftiness appealed to the bothy men who thought it was on account of his being on the run, as indeed they were. Within the space of two years he had shopped every illicit distiller around the Cromarty Firth and then south as far as Fort William at the southern tip of Loch Ness. You might say he was the original Loch Ness Monster – far too shifty to be real. It was when he started snitching on the gaugers that the double subterfuge made things too hot for him. He was attempting to make his way back home across the Isle of Skye when he encountered a still in full production on the shores of Loch Harport. He could find no one to tell and began gibbering to himself out loud. He was overheard and set adrift in a small dinghy with enough provisions to get him to the Hebrides. Whether he ever made it no one knows and it turned out that no one cared. If he ever did make it home everyone had been cleared out anyway and he could never snitch on anyone again.

The story was that they used to walk with the coffin. The coffin had handles on the side, as they do. They'd stop for a rest and put the coffin down and two men would take their place. The two men in the middle went to the front and two new ones would come in at the back. So they were constantly changing. When they stopped they would have a fairly large dram with the cortège behind. On one occasion they got to the graveside and found they'd left the coffin behind on the road somewhere!

Jim McEwan, Bowmore distillery

TAMDHU Railway STATION Distillery SHOP and TOURIST ATTRACTION

CANOEISTS

PLEASE BE DISCREET
WHILST
CHANGING CLOTHING
IN THIS AREA

Aberfeldy

Aberfeldy distillery was established in 1898, on the road to Perth, on the south side of the River Tay. Fresh spring water is taken from the nearby Pitilie Burn to produce this unique single malt with its distinctive peaty nose, its rasping good looks, energy-saving panty hose . . . what? And 43% volume beyond the thighs of the most prodigious siren and only 15 years old – goddammit! What a whisky!! – and it's got a kind of squirrel on it. Very light, not unlike Caol Ila, a similar kind of label, and a similar kind of squirrel. The classic kind to instil confidence and an expensive response

ABERFELDY Distillery — PERTHSHIRE

from a potential customer. It was at this point that I realised that all distilleries have managers. It took me back to the time when I was working in Woolworths as a trainee manager, and I found myself struggling on the floor of the stockroom with the manager himself, who did not like me, or that is the impression I got, for we were locked in mortal combat amongst collapsing storage shelves. It was at that point that I was asked to leave. I finished making the refuse paper bail I had started, dusted myself off, left as quietly as I dared, and started all over again.

MORRISON'S GLEN GARIOCH Distillery Old MELDRUM, Aberdeenshire

Glen Garioch

Old Meldrum is the village attached to and developed around the distillery known as Glen Garioch. It has a quaint air of old worldliness about it and a terrible chip shop. The distillery is particularly interesting in that the heat generated during the distilling process is not wasted but piped through a huge greenhouse complex throughout the year. Tomato plants are trained horizontally along tracks supported by intermittent strings. This enables the plants to grow many yards away from their richly fed rooting system to sustain anything up to 60 bunches of tomatoes per plant. A truly Scottish characteristic in action.

The manager is a warm and hospitable man who allowed my nephew and his crew to film whatever they may. They had come to see me on the job and film me in action.

Unfortunately they had left by the time Ian Fyfe decided to break into song (see page 6).

We tried the 10, 15 and 21 year-old single malts. Sublime unctions culminating in the softer 21 year-old. The 15 year-old hid the heart of an athlete and was at optimum state for drinking. Age too can blunt the true nature of a single malt.

Glen Garioch – Founded 1797 by Ingram Lamb and Co. 1840, bought by John Manson then J.F. Thompson of Leith. 2 maltings – barley was grown in the neighbourhood. Peat kiln. Mash tun 14 feet diameter. Wort in underback – 3,000 gallons. 3 washbacks – 5,000 gallons. Wash charger of oak to serve the stills. Wash still 1,900 gallons. Worm tub 40 feet long and 5 feet deep. Low wines still – 1,500 gallons. 12 men employed. Local peat. Water from Fircock Hill. 50,000 gallons per year.

Longmorn Distillery

Fettercairn Distillery, Kincardine Highlands east ... and Boswell the Aberdeen Angus — Ralph Steadman

Fettercairn

Traditionally it never needed many to make it – one to distil and one to look out for the gauger . . .

It is one of the oldest distilleries and went legal in 1824. Its water comes from high up in the Cairngorms and it is situated on flat lands, near the North Esk river. It is now very high-tech and, true to its tradition, requires practically no one to run it.

The stories are legion about how people escape with spirit from distilleries. The long thin tube in the trousers, for example, or the guy who brought a bottle of milk in with him every day. He always went home with the bottle full, never drank it. Actually it was filled with whisky when he went home, but you would never know, because it was painted white on the inside.

Anonymous

A delicious, fine, strong, rippling muscularity defines this most famous of single malts for me. Sometimes, I start thinking that it is over-praised, yet, grudgingly, I have to acknowledge its pedigree. It is one of Scotland's flagship exports and has enjoyed the best of everything for so long that I often resist buying it, since it does all right without my patronage. However, when I do buy a bottle, it always lives beyond the opinion that settles upon me like misty rain, and I have to admit how fine it really is.

"The GLENLIVET" Distillery, Ballindalloch,

...ire (SPEYSIDE)   Ralph STEADman 9.

4 Smugglers and Guagers of Terse and Ruthless PEDIGREE

Men and women of gritty and brutal intensity ran amok at the turn of the 19th century. Overnight it went from Scottleland to Bottleland and the heather heaved with the feverish activity of steaming hideyholes, wherever a pot still could be secreted and hidden within minutes to avoid discovery.

SHORTAS LARGYBEG DROON, though slow-witted, used his slow ways to invent a system of distillation that was continuous, saved time and which he kept going for 45 years though he never any of the whisky. That was perhaps the nature of his slowness. The whole process was arranged along the bank of a fast-flowing burn above Loch Snizart along the western coast of Skye. Water would go in through a catch funnel at one end and mix with his own mucky brown wort. He would then boil it, ferment it, percolate it like coffee through his tube labyrinth, moofle it off as alcoholic steam into an antechamber, and cool it through a submerged zigzag worm before belching it out into the burn again further down the glen. Those folk using the burn below his still walked in a perpetual stupor and never knew a sober day from birth to death. Shortas Droon pre-dated Robert Stein and Aeneas Coffey with their 'patent' continuous still inventions by at least 26 years, though Droon was never credited with anything but slowness.

WEE TOMMY WETKNEDDLIE did absolutely nothing for the smuggling trade but claimed blood ties with everyone. An inveterate liar, he told touring parties anything they wanted to believe in exchange for a wee dram. He had his uses, though, since he would often blab all manner of lies to roaming excise men who would take him at his word and stagger off in another direction on the strength of a new clue. He wore a patch only to elicit more sympathy and for dramatic effect, though it was, in fact, his purse in which he kept the King's shilling, though never found a need to spend it. He claimed he gave his sporran to Bonnie Prince Charlie to express his generosity and loyalty.

JOCKLER BARLEYCORN MCVAIG grew the finest barley and from it produced the silkiest peatreek though he was a farmer first who loved the land and a still man second because he loved the drink. He could only grow the best barley when he was drunk and only got poetry out of a still when he was gravestone sober. His wife Ellie would only have him in the house when he was between those two states – 'when the man can gae me a sensible leer', she said. The gaugers never caught him. He was far too drunk to talk to when he tilled his land and when he was at his still he was far too sober to let a gauger catch him at it. He was known as a well-rounded fellow.

62

GAY GORDON FANBUGGERY was never told whether she was a man or a woman. The product of relentless inbreeding, Gay was weaned as a boy since the Fanbuggerys had already got twelve daughters. Gay grew as tough as a man in a skirt and learned to arm wrestle and drink with the smugglers who frequented the Tilted Wig on the Isle of Muck. The only time she used her feminine charms was when there came a visit from the gaugers which has to be said was rare. As they came ashore Gay would stand full square on the end of the jetty, flex her muscles enticingly and spit on the capstan until they turned around and went away. She was much praised by all smugglers for what they referred to as her art of seduction. In this way she fulfilled her womanhood without losing her heart to any man.

PIPEWORM LOLA CLATTIE was courted by many a still man for her amazing pipework. She could magically wind a worm through any burn, transforming it into what appeared to be virtual undergrowth to a passer-by. Many an angler has cursed her very name on getting his tackle tangled with Lola's mangled wangle pipe network – a miracle of plumbing ingenuity in perpetuity . . . She was patronised by royalty who commissioned her to design the pipework for the organ in the private chapel at Balmoral.

PEABROCH GWENNIE BAGDHU distilled her wort through bagpipes and played pure Pibroch pipe music as the vapours condensed. She believed that the very soul of Scotland entered the spirit as it passed through her beloved instrument. She had her own technique of playing, developed over the years through her suck-blow counterpoint harmonic drone and scalic progressions which vibrated through the vapours creating a cacophony of pure liquid music.

Nobody else can produce Highland Park whisky. You could set up a distillery in, say, Tunbridge Wells, get the same kind of barley, import the water from Orkney, make the mash, ferment it, distil it in the same-shaped stills, put it in the same barrels, let it mature for the same length of time, and it would still taste like kangaroo piss. You will never be able to explain that chemically.

Anthony Troon, Journalist

SHERLOCK MACBHU was a master of disguise and many swore he could blend with the landscape into virtual invisibility. But none missed his eyes or his socks, only when it was too late and he was upon them. His eyes were bloodshot orange and his socks were adorned with the fur of white rabbits. Macbhu rarely slept – he could not, knowing that even one bothy bubbled and glooped profit into the smuggler's palm. Finally he did go to sleep on the banks of Loch Ness after his ten thousandth arrest, and 'tis said that his ghost is about when the mists rise and the banks of the Loch are chequered in tartan.

BLACK ANGUS GLENBLACKLAS took no quarter from anyone nor did he give any. His heart was blacker than his name. His glowering black eyebrows were enough to strike the very curse of black granite into the soul of any man. He was as bald as he was black and he hid his only guilty secret beneath a glowing lock of black eyebrow swept over his pate and tied with a black bow. He carried a blackguard's stick with the head of a bald vulture on its top which he brandished like a claymore. The vulture's beak could transform a useful copper still into a worthless colander in a matter of minutes with a thousand 'holes of enlightenment' as he used to refer to them. He is still alive and lives in Blackheath.

MUCKLEY MCSHONACH, one of the many excise officers who ultimately fell victim to the enticements and rare temptations of some of the finest illicit malts that were ever made. Some were undrinkable and their makers would feel the full force of Muckley's Law, while some of the truly classic malts became their bargaining chips of survival for those who were artists of their craft. Men like Muckley McShonach could never resist a tempting wee dram – 'though only a wee one, mind.' There was much work to be done. The bothy boys were forever busy. Muckley finally expired like an oil tanker in a massive fireball of inflammable vapours when he fell backwards into a hidden bothy before the very eyes of the smugglers themselves who never drank another drop to his memory.

There's no duty on a shotgun!
Anon